AMERICAN PLACES
From Vision to Reality

The White House

by Kevin Blake

Consultant:
Nicole Hemmer, Visiting Research Associate
Miller Center of Public Affairs
University of Virginia
Charlottesville, Virginia

BEARPORT
PUBLISHING

New York, New York

Credits

Cover, © Orhan Cam/Shutterstock; 2–3, © andriano.cz/Shutterstock; 4, © North Wind Picture Archives/Alamy; 5L, tinyurl.com/hrvdqcv/Public Domain; 5R, tinyurl.com/h9jj98c/Public Domain; 6, tinyurl.com/zfhyyzn/Public Domain; 7T, © White House Collection/White House Historical Association; 7B, tinyurl.com/jjsapg8/Public Domain; 8, © Jose Ignacio Soto/Shutterstock; 9, © Granger, NYC; 10L, © Everett Historical/Shutterstock; 10R, WHHA/Public Domain; 11T, © Courtesy of the Maryland Historical Society, 1976.88.3; 11B, © Jean Housen/CC BY-SA 3.0; 12, © North Wind Pictures Archive/Alamy; 13L, © White House Collection/White House Historical Association; 13R, © Everett Historical/Shutterstock; 14TL, tinyurl.com/jljgp8h/Public Domain; 14TR, tinyurl.com/jnljfws/Public Domain; 14B, © White House Historical Association; 15, © White House Historical Association; 16L, tinyurl.com/jh3fulk/Public Domain; 16R, © Marcnorman/Dreamstime; 17, © Everett Historical/Shutterstock; 18–19, tinyurl.com/hn8e63m/Public Domain; 19BR, © White House Collection/White House Historical Association; 20T, © Everett Historical/Shutterstock; 20B, © Everett Historical/Shutterstock; 21T, Library of Congress; 21B, © FPWing/Shutterstock; 22L, tinyurl.com/zl6kky7/Public Domain; 22R, Library of Congress; 23, © Everett Collection Inc/Alamy; 24, U.S. National Archives/tinyurl.com/zg5oyo5/Public Domain; 25, U.S. National Archives/tinyurl.com/gszmr59/Public Domain; 26L, © Everett Collection Inc/Alamy; 26R, © WDC Photos/Alamy; 27, © Everett Collection Inc/Alamy; 28–29, © imagedj/Shutterstock; 28–29 (background), © robert_s/Shutterstock; 31, © Orhan Cam/Shutterstock; 32, © Liz Van Steenburgh/Shutterstock.

Publisher: Kenn Goin
Senior Editor: Joyce Tavolacci
Creative Director: Spencer Brinker
Design: The Design Lab
Photo Researcher: Editorial Directions, Inc.

Library of Congress Cataloging-in-Publication Data

Names: Blake, Kevin, 1978– author.
Title: The White House / by Kevin Blake.
Description: New York, New York : Bearport Publishing Company, Inc., 2017. | Series: American
  places: from vision to reality | Includes bibliographical references and index. | Audience: Age 7–12
Identifiers: LCCN 2016012277 (print) | LCCN 2016012627 (ebook) | ISBN 9781944102425
  (library binding) | ISBN 9781944997151 (ebook)
Subjects: LCSH: White House (Washington, D.C.)—Juvenile literature. | Washington (D.C.)—
  Buildings, structures, etc.—Juvenile literature.
Classification: LCC F204.W5 B58 2017 (print) | LCC F204.W5 (ebook) | DDC 975.3—dc23
LC record available at http://lccn.loc.gov/2016012277

For more information, write to Bearport Publishing Company, Inc.,
45 West 21st Street, Suite 3B, New York, New York 10010.
Printed in the United States of America.

10 9 8 7 6 5 4 3 2 1

Contents

Fire!

On a warm night in August 1814, fifty British soldiers stood outside the White House in Washington, DC. It was the **War of 1812**, and the British were on the attack. Each soldier held a long pole with an oil-soaked rag on the end. The soldiers lit the rags and held the poles high in the air. One of the men shouted an order, and, all at once, the soldiers threw their flaming poles through the windows of the **majestic** house.

British soldiers setting fire to the White House in 1814

Within seconds, the White House was on fire. Nearby, a group of Americans watched in horror as flames **engulfed** the home of their president, James Madison. As the fire spread, it destroyed almost everything inside the building. If not for the heavy rain from a powerful thunderstorm later that day, the entire White House might have burned to the ground.

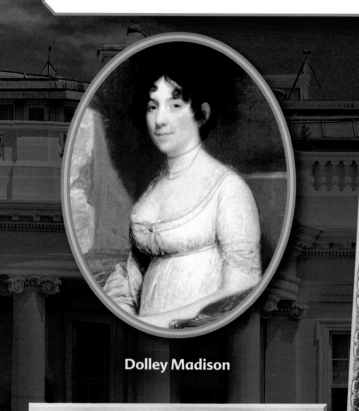
Dolley Madison

The portrait of George Washington that Dolley Madison saved

President James Madison had left the White House before the British arrived. However, his wife, Dolley, was at the house when it was under attack. Before escaping the blaze, she made sure to save a few items, including a large portrait of George Washington.

The New Capital

Not long before the British attack, there wasn't a White House or a Washington, DC. In fact, there wasn't even a United States of America! America had started as a group of British **colonies** in the 1600s. In 1775, these colonies decided they wanted to rule themselves. They fought for their **independence** from Great Britain during the Revolutionary War. In 1783, the United States of America won the war.

A painting showing a battle during the Revolutionary War (1775—1783)

This new nation would need a permanent **capital** for its new government. In 1790, a group of leaders known as the Founding Fathers decided to build the capital on a piece of land between Maryland and Virginia. They named the land Washington, DC, in honor of George Washington, the nation's first president. Now that there was a capital, the president of the United States needed a place to live.

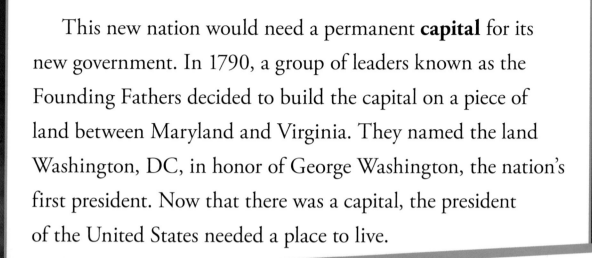

An early map of Washington, DC

In the late 1700s, the Founding Fathers helped set up the government of the United States. The group included George Washington, Thomas Jefferson, and several other men.

A House for a President

What type of house should be built for the new president? No one knew the answer because no other country had a president. In Europe, kings and queens ruled. They **inherited** their wealth and power and lived in huge, **lavish** palaces.

The Palace of Versailles was built as a home for a king in France.

The U.S. president, however, was very different from a king. He was a leader chosen by the people he would govern. The Founding Fathers believed the president's home should be much simpler than a palace. It should represent the **democratic** principles of the new country—but what exactly should the house look like? Thomas Jefferson suggested holding a contest encouraging the public to submit designs for the new house. President George Washington loved the idea.

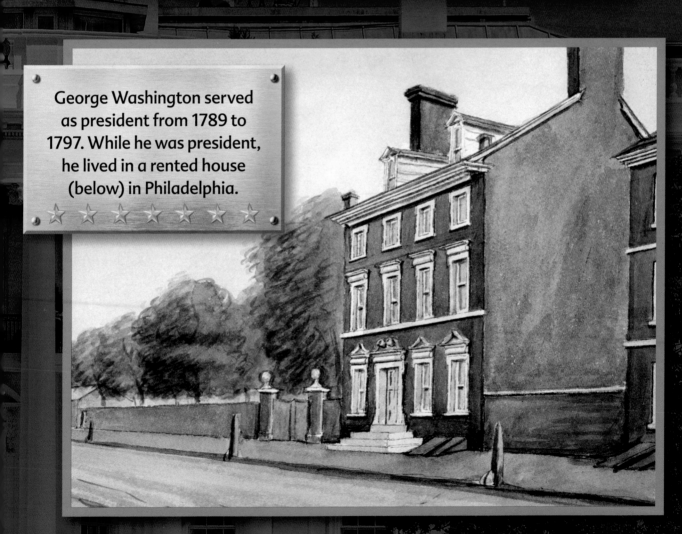

George Washington served as president from 1789 to 1797. While he was president, he lived in a rented house (below) in Philadelphia.

The Contest

In 1792, Thomas Jefferson invited people to join the contest. The winner of the competition would receive a prize of $500 or a medal—plus get the honor of designing the president's home. President Washington himself would pick the winner.

Thomas Jefferson

WASHINGTON, *in the Territory of* COLUMBIA.

A PREMIUM

OF FIVE HUNDRED DOLLARS, or a MEDAL of that value, at the option of the party, will be given by the Commissioners of the Federal Buildings, to the person who, before the fifteenth day of July next, shall produce to them the most approved PLAN, if adopted by them, for a PRESIDENT'S HOUSE, to be erected in this City. The site of the building, if the artist will attend to it, will of course influence the aspect and outline of his plan; and it's destination will point out to him the number, size, and distribution of the apartments. It will be a recommendation of any plan, if the central part of it may be detached and erected for the present, with the appearance of a complete whole, and be capable of admitting the additional parts, in future, if they shall be wanting. Drawings will be expected of the ground plats, elevations of each front, and sections through the building, in such directions as may be necessary to explain the internal structure; and an estimate of the cubic feet of brick-work composing the whole mass of the walls.

March 14, 1792. THE COMMISSIONERS.

The original advertisement for the contest to design the president's house

Washington reviewed the designs and chose one sent in by an **architect** named James Hoban. Hoban's design was simple and elegant and included four large columns along the front of the house. Washington made a few small changes to the design, including making the house bigger. Now it was time to build.

The Leinster House

Many historians think that Hoban based his design on a building called the Leinster House in Dublin, Ireland.

James Hoban's sketch for the president's home

Construction

In 1792, President Washington visited the site where the house would be built and carefully hammered four **stakes** into the muddy ground. The posts marked where the four outside walls of the new house would be built.

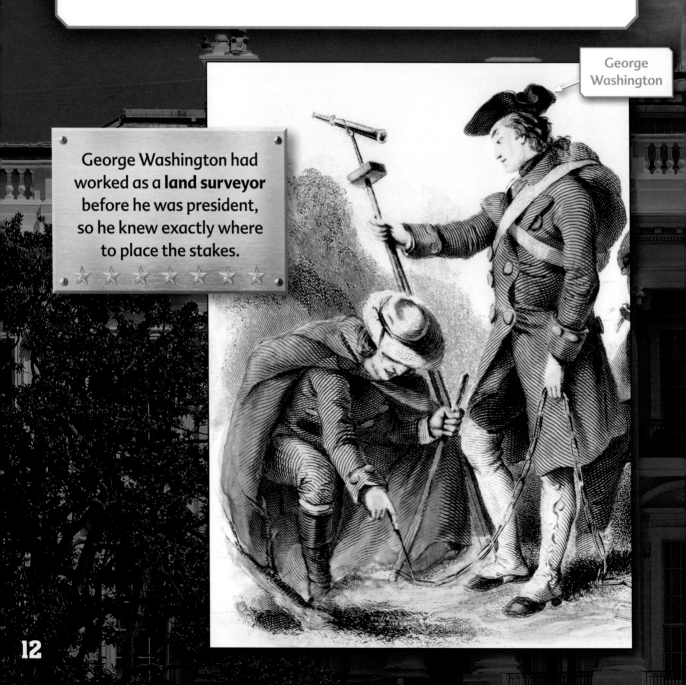

George Washington

George Washington had worked as a **land surveyor** before he was president, so he knew exactly where to place the stakes.

A lot of workers were needed to build the house, including slaves from nearby farms and **masons** from as far away as Scotland. The workers used wood and **plaster** to construct the interior of the building. They used tan-colored sandstone to build the outside walls. The builders worried that rain would seep into the **porous** stone and cause it to crack. So they covered the house with thick white paint made from salt, rice, and glue. This paint would keep the water out and give the house its famous color and name.

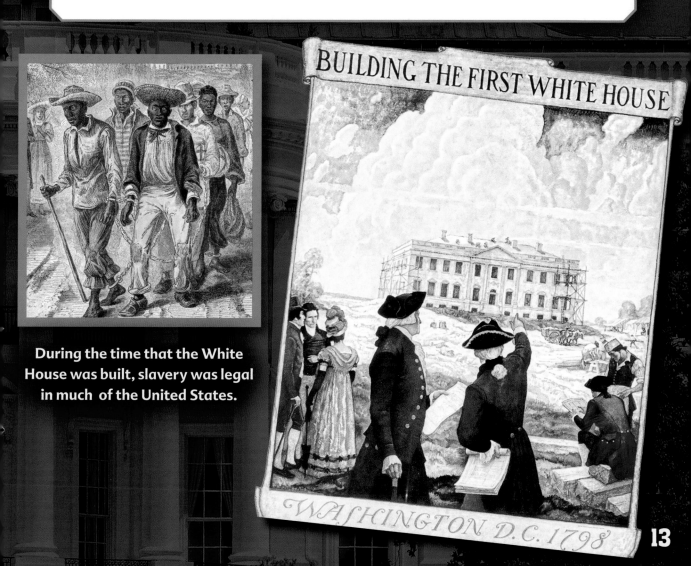

During the time that the White House was built, slavery was legal in much of the United States.

BUILDING THE FIRST WHITE HOUSE

WASHINGTON D.C. 1798

The First Family

In 1796, John Adams was elected the second U.S. president. In November 1800, after the house had been under construction for eight years, Adams and his wife Abigail moved in. However, the house was not quite finished. The front lawn was covered with building materials and mud. Inside the house, there was a huge hole where the main staircase was supposed to be. Also, fires blazed in many of the mansion's 39 fireplaces in order to dry the still wet plaster walls.

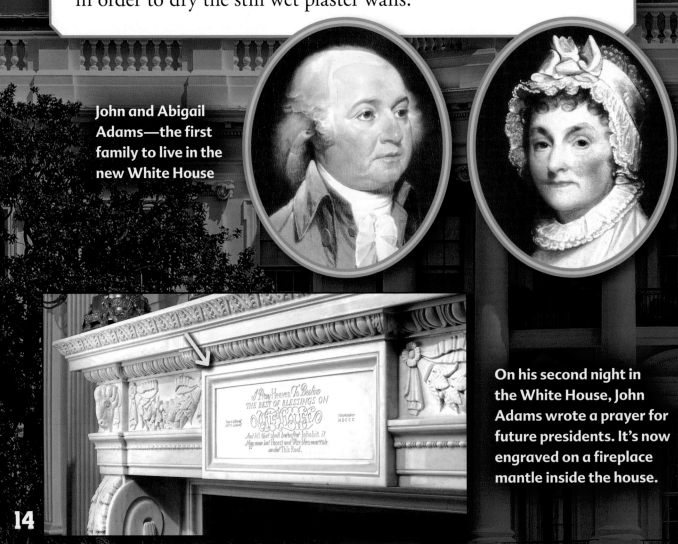

John and Abigail Adams—the first family to live in the new White House

On his second night in the White House, John Adams wrote a prayer for future presidents. It's now engraved on a fireplace mantle inside the house.

Abigail Adams wasn't happy with her new home. She thought the big house was cold and drafty. Also, she had no idea where to hang the president's laundry to dry. She thought it wasn't proper to display the president's clothes outside, so she asked her servants to hang them in the biggest room in the house, which was later called the East Room.

When the Adams's moved into the White House, some of the rooms had been wallpapered and stunk like beer—a key ingredient in the paste used to hang the paper.

This painting shows a servant hanging laundry in the East Room while Abigail Adams looks on.

A Personal Touch

John and Abigail Adams didn't live in the house for long. Just a month after they moved in, Thomas Jefferson was elected president. In 1801, Jefferson made the White House his home. He was an **amateur** architect and had lots of ideas about how to make the building more beautiful.

Thomas Jefferson was the first president to open the White House for public tours.

Before he was president, Thomas Jefferson designed and lived in this house, called Monticello, in Virginia.

President Jefferson installed two covered passageways called colonnades. He also added a stable for horses, a laundry area, and colorful gardens. Inside the house, Jefferson decorated the rooms with finely made furniture from France. By the time President James Madison moved into the house in 1809, the White House had become one of the grandest houses in the nation.

The original White House roof leaked. While he was president, Jefferson installed a new roof that kept the house dry.

Rebuilding

All the work that had been put into the White House went up in smoke when the British set fire to the building in 1814. The fire destroyed everything but the house's exterior walls, which were badly damaged but still standing. The house that had taken so much time and effort to construct had to be almost completely rebuilt.

A painting that shows the White House after the 1814 fire

James Madison, the president at the time of the fire, asked the original architect, James Hoban, to help reconstruct the White House. It took several years, but workers were able to rebuild it. When the work was finally done, the only thing left from inside the original White House was the portrait of George Washington that Dolley Madison had saved from the fire.

Workers were able to reuse parts of the **foundation** of the original White House for the new building.

Burn marks from the 1814 fire left on the White House

Making It Modern

The White House continued to change as each new president left his mark on the building. Some of the biggest changes happened when new technology was introduced. For instance, in the 1830s, President Andrew Jackson added running water and indoor plumbing to the house. Before then, people were forced to use **outhouses**. Jackson also added a special bathing room to the East Wing that featured a shower and a bath heated by a copper **boiler**.

A drawing of the
White House from 1829

Andrew Jackson

One of the biggest changes came in 1891. That's when electricity was installed in the White House. Electrical wires, lights, and on/off switches were put in every room. President Benjamin Harrison and his wife were frightened to touch the strange new switches because they feared they would get shocked!

A new electric light fixture in a White House bedroom in 1899

In 1877, a telephone was installed in the White House. The phone number was 1.

A Home Office

The White House wasn't only a home—it was also an office for the most important leader in the country. When President Theodore Roosevelt moved into the house with his wife and children in 1901, he wanted a more private place to work. In 1902, he constructed new offices in the western end of the White House. People began calling this area the West Wing.

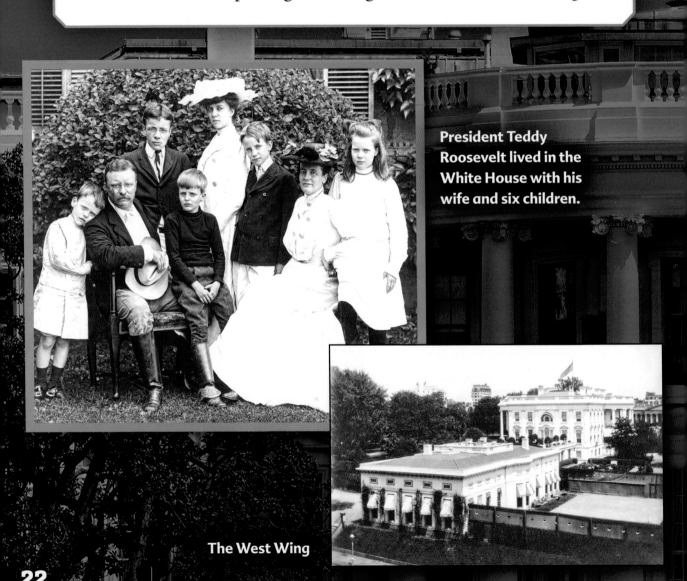

President Teddy Roosevelt lived in the White House with his wife and six children.

The West Wing

In 1909, when William Taft was president, he expanded the West Wing and built an unusual round room. Today this room is known as the Oval Office, and it's where the president makes many important decisions. Each president can decorate the office however he or she chooses. However, many use the same antique desk, which was made out of wood from an old British warship!

President John F. Kennedy and his children have some fun in the Oval Office in 1962.

Outside the Oval Office is the White House Rose Garden, planted in 1913 by Ellen Axson Wilson, wife of President Woodrow Wilson. This is where the president talks to the **press** and hosts famous visitors.

Fixer-Upper

By 1948, the White House had fallen into **disrepair**. The ceiling of the East Room was sagging almost 18 inches (46 cm) and was on the verge of collapsing. President Harry Truman even saw a piano leg crash through one of the floors! The 100-year-old wooden beams holding up the White House weren't strong enough to support the house anymore.

President Truman talking with White House architects and staff

In December 1948, President Truman decided to undertake a major **renovation** of the house. To stabilize the building, much of it was rebuilt with concrete and more than 660 tons (599 metric tons) of steel. Workers dug two new basement floors for storage and offices and also built a **bomb shelter** to keep the president safe in case of an enemy attack. The renovation took four long years, but after it was completed, the house was better and safer than ever.

Workers rebuild the State Dining Room where the president greets leaders from around the world.

President Truman also added a **balcony** that overlooks the South Lawn. President Barack Obama once said the Truman Balcony was his family's favorite spot in the whole house.

The White House Today

The White House is more than just a home and an office, it's also a place for the president and his family to have fun. Some presidents even built areas to play their favorite games. For instance, President Harry Truman built a bowling alley, and President Barack Obama constructed a basketball court.

President Richard Nixon bowling in the White House in 1971

President Barack Obama playing basketball at the White House in 2009

In addition to being the president's home, the White House is also a popular **tourist** destination. As many as 100,000 people visit the White House each month. People come from around the country—and around the world—to tour the historic building. They want to see where American history was made—and continues to be made!

First Lady Michelle Obama says hello to lucky guests on a White House tour in 2010.

You don't have to visit Washington, DC, to see the White House. You can take a virtual tour of the White House online!

The White House
BY THE NUMBERS

1790 — **1800** — **1810** — **1820**

1792
Construction of White House begins.

1800
John Adams moves into the White House. He's the first U.S. president to live in the house.

1814
The British set fire to the house.

1814–1817
The White House is rebuilt.

Length of Building: 168 feet (51 m) long

Approximate Height of Building: 70 feet (21 m)

Number of Rooms: 132

Number of Bathrooms: 35

Number of Windows: 147

Number of Doors: 412

The White House requires about 570 gallons (2,158 l) of paint to cover its outside surface.

1830

1833
President Andrew Jackson adds indoor plumbing.

1890

1891
President Benjamin Harrison installs electricity.

1900

1902
President Theodore Roosevelt begins construction on the West Wing.

1950

1948–1952
President Harry Truman renovates the White House.

Glossary

amateur (AM-uh-chur) someone who is not a professional

architect (AHR-kih-tekt) a person who designs buildings

balcony (BAL-kuh-nee) a platform on the outside of a building

boiler (BOY-lur) a tank in which water is heated or stored

bomb shelter (BOM SHEL-tur) a place, usually underground, designed to be safe from a bomb attack

capital (KAP-uh-tuhl) the city in a state or country where the government is based

colonies (KOL-uh-neez) areas that have been settled by people from another country and are ruled by that country

democratic (dem-uh-KRAT-tik) a form of government in which people vote to choose their leaders

disrepair (diss-ri-PAIR) bad condition

engulfed (en-GULFD) surrounded or swallowed up by something

foundation (foun-DAY-shuhn) the base on which a building rests

independence (in-di-PEN-duhnss) freedom

inherited (in-HAIR-uh-tid) received from a parent

land surveyor (LAND sur-VAY-ur) someone whose job is to find out the size and shape of a piece of land

lavish (LAV-ish) extravagant

majestic (muh-JESS-tik) showing impressive beauty

masons (MAY-suhns) people who build things with stone, brick, or cement

outhouses (OUT-hou-ziz) buildings that are located outside and contain a toilet

plaster (PLAS-tur) a mixture of water and tiny bits of rock that hardens as it dries

porous (POHR-uhs) full of holes that allow water or air to enter

press (PRESS) reporters and other people who work for newspapers and television stations

renovation (REN-uh-vay-shun) the act of rebuilding and fixing

stakes (STAYKS) sticks or posts that mark a spot

tourist (TOOR-ist) a person who visits a place for pleasure

War of 1812 (WAWR uhv 1812) a military conflict between the United States and Great Britain that lasted from 1812 to 1815

Bibliography

Grove, Noel. *Inside the White House: Stories From the World's Most Famous Residence.* Washington, DC: National Geographic (2013).

Monkman, Betty C. *The White House: Its Historic Furnishings & First Families.* New York: Abbeville Press (2014).

The National Park Service, President's Park (White House): www.nps.gov/whho/

The White House Historical Association: www.whitehousehistory.org

Read More

Grace, Catherine. *The White House: An Illustrated History.* New York: Scholastic (2003).

Stine, Megan. *Where Is the White House?* New York: Grosset & Dunlap (2015).

Learn More Online

To learn more about the White House, visit:
www.bearportpublishing.com/AmericanPlaces

Index

About the Author

Kevin Blake lives in Providence, Rhode Island, with his wife, Melissa, and son, Sam. He's lucky to have visited the White House!